MODERN LIFE STOICISM

No More Uncontrolled Emotions: Learn to Understand Yourself, Master Mind Control, Be Your Own Coach and Handle Though Situations, Even When it Seems to Overcome You

Table of Contents

Introduction 5

Chapter 1: Understanding Stoicism 7
   Ancient Greek School of Philosophy 7
   The Purpose for Stoicism in Society 8
   The Goal of Stoicism 10
   Why Stoicism Is Not Emotional Avoidance 11
   How Stoicism Relates to Modern Daily Living 12

Chapter 2: Mental Toughness 14
   Why Mental Toughness Matters 14
   Developing Your Mental Clarity 16
   Learning to Remain Unbiased 18
   Rationally Responding to Passionate Emotions 20
   Building Mental Resiliency 21
   Maintaining Your Mental Toughness in Challenging Times 23

Chapter 3: Discipline of Self 26
   Accepting Yourself 26
   Accepting Things Beyond Yourself 28
   Maintaining Virtue and Kindness 29
   Making Peace with Your Past 31
   Overcoming Procrastination and Distractions 32
   Moving in Alignment with Your Goals 34

Chapter 4: Discipline of Action 37
   Controlling Your Emotional Passion and Expression 38
   Acting in an Ethical Manner 39
   Solving Your Problems Effectively 41
   Acting with Discipline in Relationships 42

Moving Towards Professional Goals Ethically 43

Chapter 5: Achieving the Goal of Stoicism 45
Understanding the Goal of Modern Stoicism 45
Advice from Stoics 46
Daily Mindfulness Practices 49
A Morning Meditation for Stoicism 51
Philosophical Diaries 53
Studying the Art of Stoicism 54
Endurance Training 55

Chapter 6: Daily Application of Stoicism 58
Knowing Your True Freedom 58
The Circle of Influence and the Circle of Concern 59
Reframing Your Attitude on Death 60
Growing Comfortable in Discomfort 61
Recreating Yourself as a Person 62
Embodying Your Own Philosophies 63
Always Work Towards Your Personal Mission 64
Be a Student of Life 65
Create Happiness, Don't Dream of It 65
Learn How to Be Present 66
Always Take 100% Responsibility for Yourself 67
Grow Beyond Materialism 69
Be of Service to Others 69
Embody the Lighter Side of Life 70

Conclusion 72

Introduction

Throughout this book, I am going to share with you the best ways that you can harness and develop stoicism and use it in your daily life. From your relationships to your career, you are going to discover just what it takes to really change your life from the inside out and experience massive shifts as a result. I realize that changes are not something that can happen overnight; it happens gradually. But I am confident that if you begin applying the skills that I teach you right here in this very book that you will be able to start experiencing massive transformations quickly. As you continue applying these skill, you will continue to experience greater changes and transformations as you grow through life with the inner strength needed to overcome anything that you may have to face.

I encourage you to realize that your transformation is going to come from two significant places: understanding and consistency. Make sure that you take the time to fully understand and comprehend the concepts that I am sharing with you and that they make sense to you as you read through this book. That way, when it comes to discovering how you can apply these very techniques into your own life, you can do so in a complete and well-rounded manner. Once you have discovered exactly how to apply them, you are going to need to apply them consistently so that you can continue experiencing changes. As they say, "Rome wasn't built in a day, but they were laying bricks every hour." Change is not something that is achieved in one leap, but as long as you continue working towards your desires, then plenty can be accomplished.

You may be wondering what stoicism is exactly. Perhaps you have heard of the term a few times before but you weren't clear on what it was, or maybe this is your first time hearing it and you have never even considered that it might be a thing. So, before we dive in, I want to make sure that you have a clear understanding of just what it is that you are about to learn for the duration of the time that we are going to spend together! After all, your time is important, and you want to make sure that you are investing it into something that is actually going to help you have a major impact on your life.

Stoicism, according to the dictionary, is "the endurance of pain or hardship without a display of feelings and without complaint." On a surface level, this might sound somewhat harsh and outdated since we are currently living amongst a time where emotions are highly praised and are encouraged in most situations. While I am not saying that emotions should ever be discouraged or bottled up, what I am saying is that there is an appropriate manner in which emotions should be handled, especially in certain situations. By learning about stoicism, you develop a sense of emotional intelligence that enables you to both experience and express your emotions while also gaining the benefits of not letting your emotions take over you. Despite stoicism being a form of emotional intelligence, you should realize that this is only one element of what stoicism truly is. This particular philosophy not only educates you on key aspects of emotional intelligence, but also supports you in developing mental toughness, resiliency, and the ability to be more accepting of both yourself and others in your life. By embodying all of these elements of stoicism, you can develop a sense of maturity that supports you in experiencing a fuller life both personally and professionally as you equip yourself with the proper tools to navigate any situation you may face in life.

If you are ready to begin embracing the power of stoicism and learning about how you can develop it and apply it to your own life, then I would say it is time that we begin! Please take a moment to prepare yourself for what might be one of the most life-changing experiences you will ever endure. And, of course, be sure to enjoy!

Chapter 1: Understanding Stoicism

You now have a basic understanding of what stoicism is in regard to it being a form of emotional intelligence and mental resiliency, but you still do not truly understand the full concept of stoicism. Stoicism is a rather complex concept that actually has a rich history in ancient Greece. To truly understand what it is, how it works, and what purpose it is designed to achieve, you need to look at it from the earliest developments of its philosophy. From there, you can begin to understand why this particular skill is so valuable, and how it continues to relate to the modern world even though we have evolved so much from these early days.

In this chapter, we are going to explore important concepts around stoicism, such as its Greek roots and how it relates to modern-day living. You are also going to develop an understanding of what the real goal of stoicism is and why it is actually an incredibly valuable tool despite the fact that it was poorly executed for many years in our recent history. This way, you can understand exactly how stoicism relates to you and why it is such an important concept for you to grasp and comprehend.

Ancient Greek School of Philosophy

Stoicism was originally introduced to society back in the ancient Greek school of philosophy by a gentleman named Zeno of Citium. It was originally founded in c. 300 B.C.E. Inspired by Cynics, Zeno was a disciple of Socrates and spent his life as a philosopher, attempting to understand the purpose of life and the meaning of various human realities and experiences. One of Zeno's most influential followers was named Chrysippus, and it was Chrysippus who was actually responsible for molding the philosophy that is now known as stoicism.

The majority of scholars who educated themselves on Greek philosophy and stoicism typically divided the history of stoicism into three different phases: early Stoa, middle Stoa, and late Stoa. Early Stoa was the initial development of stoicism as founded by Zeno in his school of philosophy. The latter two phases were followed up by both the Greeks and the Romans who continued to try and understand the concepts of stoicism and develop upon it, molding it into modern-day stoicism. It was during the latter phase where Romans truly fostered the idea of stoicism, with some of the Empires praising it and cherishing it and others persecuting it.

Back in these early days, stoicism was a philosophy that was supposed to teach individuals how to develop self-control so that they could overcome destructive emotions. True stoicism was not designed to encourage people to extinguish or ignore their emotions, but instead to discover how they could transform those emotions through the voluntary absence of worldly pleasures, also known as "Asceticism". As an ancient leader, this would mean that you would have the self-control to feel emotions of anger or jealousy without immediately acting upon them so as to seek immediate worldly pleasure through revenge. Instead, one would willingly abstain from the pursuit of pleasure and find a resolution that worked in a less intense or cruel manner.

The usage of stoicism was intended to support a person in developing a clearer sense of judgment, a deeper sense of inner calmness, and the freedom from their suffering. It was not implemented as merely a skill or a belief system but instead was used as a way of life by those who wished to implement it into their daily living habits and rituals. Stoicism, then, was about an ethical way of living that would enable people to experience their emotions without immediately acting upon them in excessive or sometimes animalistic ways. Some argue that it was fundamental in our ability to evolve further as species to be able to live in a more civilized manner amongst other humans.

The Purpose for Stoicism in Society

Stoicism is a rather complex tool that can be used to elevate people out of many varieties of worldly suffering. To get a deeper understanding of how, we are going to look at the many ways that stoicism can help end needless suffering and promote a more positive and healthy society in general. The same concepts that allowed stoicism to be so powerful and helpful back in ancient Greece and Rome are the same reasons as to why it continues to be such a powerful concept in modern society.

Perhaps, one of the biggest benefits ancient civilizations gained from stoicism was the development of emotional intelligence which leads to individuals being able to train themselves into choosing between emotional and rational thought responses. This may have been highly fundamental in our history by preventing humans from having aggressive and violent reactions to their emotions so that they could begin having more intentional and thoughtful responses. For example, say an ancient Greek *archon*, or ruler, had been slighted by someone and experienced an intense burst of anger because he was angry that someone would defy his absolute power. Without stoicism, that ruler may simply sentence the individual to death and have him murdered publicly as a display of absolute power and to warn others off of wronging him. On an individual level, this may lead to deep inner feelings of trauma and guilt, particularly if the *archon* later regretted his decision and wished that he had spared the life of the other individual. This was not an uncommon experience back in the days of ancient Greece, where people would murder just about anyone out of anger, even their loved ones. Obviously, this leads to intense experiences of guilt and shame, and deep feelings of grief and despair which would lead to intense worldly suffering within the person who had experienced the aggressive outrage. With stoicism, the ruler would experience the intense anger but choose to experience it passively, or in a way that allows them to recognize and experience it but not act in such an intense and violent manner. As a result, they would avoid the needless endurance of guilt, shame, grief, and despair at the loss of an individual at their own hand.

While intense violent outbursts are not as common in the modern world, they still can happen from time to time, and they can still have just as negative of an impact on both parties as they ever did. While we do not exercise things like the death penalty or intense violent punishments like we once did, there are still many unkind things that people do as a way to exercise revenge against those who have upset or wronged them. Embodying stoicism can help prevent needless suffering by helping you not have such intense emotional outbursts towards those around you, thus allowing you and the other person to avoid unnecessary feelings of suffering.

Another way that stoicism can avoid feelings of suffering is by teaching a healthy detachment from feelings of loss, lack, or desperation. In both ancient and modern societies, many people have lived in conditions that are often deemed less than ideal by those living in them and by those living around them. Unfortunately, no real solutions have yet been presented to help every person in every society live a comfortable life free of any worldly sufferings such as poverty or hunger. While stoicism cannot earn you a greater income or feed a hungry tummy, it can prevent you from experiencing intense victimhood from these types of worldly experiences. In that detachment, you can see yourself as being separate from your worldly suffering and able to still experience joy and happiness despite the troubles that are happening in your life. This may not be equal to increasing your income or finding food during hungry times, but it can prevent you from experiencing these with the added stress of inner suffering and pain. For some people, the liberation from their own inner suffering is enough for them to find a solution to increase their income or find food to eat.

There are many additional types of worldly sufferings that people may have and have faced throughout the history of humankind. Stoicism may not always be the worldly answer to helping you get your hands on the resources that you need to liberate yourself from challenges, but it can certainly be a powerful tool in helping you prevent additional suffering. As such, stoicism can be a profound way to help you make the best out of any situation and use yourself as your own best tool in helping you to discover and experience a better way of living.

The Goal of Stoicism

The goal of stoicism is ultimately to end the experience of inner suffering by providing individuals with the freedom from passion (or anguish) through the pursuit of reason. By fostering the ability to be objective, unemotional, and mentally clear regarding any worldly challenges that a person may face, they can gain a greater sense of control over their worldly responses and avoid further suffering. So, in a very basic sense, the goal is to end unnecessary inner suffering in individuals through stoicism.

When you choose to embrace stoicism in your own life, your goal is not to experience no suffering at all but to detach from worldly suffering and eliminate the development of unnecessary suffering. So, instead of experiencing a great amount of anger and acting on it, thus also bringing about a great amount of guilt, you would instead experience anger and make the inner choice to experience it passively. Through this passive experience, you can overcome the feelings of guilt and shame and avoid further unnecessary suffering from within.

Of course, developing stoicism is not the easiest and most natural thing in a society that often uses shame and guilt as a way to pressure people into doing certain things throughout their lives. However, learning how to embrace stoicism will allow you to teach yourself to intentionally and willingly step back from the unnecessary suffering of these pressures and begin to take more control over yourself and your inner emotional experiences. This way, you can start experiencing the world around you more objectively and with more control over what your actual experience is, rather than feeling pushed around by the society around you.

Why Stoicism Is Not Emotional Avoidance

In recent Western history, a form of "skill" was being taught that educated people on the importance of avoiding their emotions so that they could go through life without the needless suffering of emotions. In this way, philosophies like stoicism were somewhat extorted to attempt to pressure people into accepting the often unfair realities that were being dealt with them by their superiors. Bosses, for example, would encourage an extorted form of stoicism to their employees to avoid having employees that would complain and attempt to revolt against the system in favor of staying quiet, calm, and compliant. This was taught on such a wide-scale level that to this day, many elders that continue to live in our modern world experience intense challenges when it comes to expressing or experiencing any form of emotion in a positive and healthy manner.

Anytime we discuss something like stoicism, which is the willful abstinence from intense emotional reactions, it is important that we also recognize that it is not about the *avoidance* of emotions altogether.

Instead, it is about recognizing and experiencing emotions but intentionally choosing to address them more constructively and productively. This is why stoicism is often related to emotional intelligence: because it supports you in choosing reasonable and rational decisions over emotional ones.

Exercising stoicism in the modern world, free of the exploitation of those who attempted to profit and benefit off of others' complete lack of emotions, does not mean living your life void of emotions. Rather, it means living your life in harmony with your emotions and learning how to exercise them and use them in a way that empowers you but refrains from you making irrational decisions that lead to further suffering later on. In this way, your emotions, which are an important part of your human experience, continue to be honored and valued, but they do not become a hindrance for your ability to experience a positive Earthly life.

How Stoicism Relates to Modern Daily Living

The modern world is heavily driven by stress, which can be filled with unnecessary amounts of pressure and overwhelming emotions. If you live in modern-day society, chances are that you can pick apart many pieces of your daily life that are filled with stress, overwhelming emotions, and pressure from things that are considered normal or standard in modern living. For example, you might find that having to wake up early to go to a career you do not really enjoy can be stressful. Aside from work, there are many other everyday stresses that people face in their lives, too: traffic, not enough time to get everything done, messy homes, overwhelmed schedules, feeling obligated to spend time with people they may not like, and so forth. Many parts of our modern lives are plagued by stress which can lead to emotions like anger, jealousy, resentment, disappointment, guilt, shame, and other painful emotions that resemble suffering.

By learning how to apply stoicism into your everyday life, especially in the modern world, you can learn how to begin experiencing freedom from these types of suffering so that you can enjoy more freedom in your daily life. Through stoicism, you can detach from the feelings of frustration in traffic, stress in going to work, or jealousy in following people on social media who flaunt the things that you wish you had in your own life. You also allow yourself to develop mental toughness and resiliency so that you can face challenging experiences in your life, including challenging emotional experiences, without such intense feelings of suffering attached to your experiences.

As you will learn throughout this book, there are many ways that true stoicism can continue to serve us in our modern world. By embracing these methods and building your mental toughness and your ability to choose reasonable thinking over emotional thinking, you can start making decisions for yourself that will improve your quality of living. As such, your suffering associated with stress and other stress-related emotions will begin to minimize as you begin enjoying a more peaceful and positive life.

Chapter 2: Mental Toughness

The first step in becoming more stoic is learning how to build mental toughness, as mental toughness is a key tool in helping you overcome emotional responses to life. When you develop your mental toughness, you enable yourself to have the mental strength required to recognize emotional experiences and rationally think your way through the process. You also equip yourself with the tool that you need to overcome challenges without feeling defeated and allowing yourself to wallow into a victim mentality.

In this chapter, you are going to begin developing your own mental toughness so that you can begin developing the strength required to navigate challenging situations without feeling so overwhelmed and overcome by emotions. This way, you can start laying the foundation for your own personal ability to detach from challenging emotional situations and choose to passively experience your emotions in a way that reduces your personal suffering. As you go through this chapter, make sure that you understand that developing mental toughness may sound easy on paper, but in all reality, it is not always as easy as it may sound. In a society that is plagued by stress and stress-related emotional struggles, mental illness and mental chaos or overwhelming emotions are extremely common and all of these can lead to it taking longer for you to develop your mental toughness. Realize that your goal here is not to suddenly develop a "thicker skin," but instead to start understanding and enforcing the practices associated with mental toughness so that you can begin seeing results from your practice. If you remain consistent and practice these tools to the best of your ability, then in due time, you will begin experiencing all of the benefits of mental toughness. While it may not be an immediate change of pace, it will be one that is certainly worth your while, and that will pave the way for you to have many more positive experiences going forward.

Why Mental Toughness Matters

When it comes to developing stoicism, or the capacity to approach challenging emotional matters with intention and focus, mental toughness is the foundation of your practice because it equips you with the strength to control your mind. Our minds are incredibly powerful tools that have the capacity to support us or hinder us in achieving the things that we desire in life, depending on how we are using them. Many people never intentionally take control over their minds and live their entire lives being victimized by their mental processes. This often happens because people do not realize that their minds are only working instinctively and with the intention of producing survival: our minds have the capacity to be used for great things, but they do not naturally do so. The people who achieve great things have developed mental toughness by developing and harnessing the tools required to actually take control over their minds and make a difference.

See, the average human mind values pleasure over anything else. Pleasure, or feelings of positive emotions and sensations, gives the mind the belief that we are experiencing something positive and that is friendly to our survival. When we experience something that is not pleasurable, it is not believed to be supportive of our survival, and therefore the mind is either neutral or negative towards it in favor of something more pleasurable. As a result, we will often instinctively behave in ways that please us, even if the acquisition of that pleasure seems strange or uncomfortable in and of itself. A basic example of this is seen with procrastination: often people procrastinate because it is more pleasurable to do nothing or relax than it is to actually engage in the task that they are putting off. Once procrastination begins to produce stress, it stops becoming pleasurable, so the person jumps into the task and tries to accomplish it rapidly to eliminate the stress and come back to the point of pure pleasure.

The problem with the human mind favoring pure pleasure is that it can be so sneaky in how it works on a subconscious level that many people have no idea what is actually driving their pleasure-seeking behaviors. To them, their behaviors may be normal or natural, and the belief that anything should be done in any other way is unnatural and uncomfortable. They may begin to produce mental beliefs or protests to justify why *they* are incapable of changing their ways when really it is just their human mind attempting to protect its access to pleasure.

When you develop mental toughness, you learn how to put off pleasure by delaying gratification through mental skills that allow you to see the benefits in doing so. These skills are developed in a way that allows you to take control over your mind and consciously control the way that pleasure is acquired so that you are not acquiring it through ways that actually increases displeasure later on. You do so by developing tools that are capable of increasing your conscious control over your mind, such as clarity, the ability to be unbiased, the capacity to exercise rational thinking, and mental resiliency. The more you develop these skills, the stronger they become and the easier it is for you to rely on them even when times are challenging. As a result, you are able to experience greater mental toughness which will pave the way for the rest of your development of stoicism.

Developing Your Mental Clarity

The first step in developing mental toughness is developing your mental clarity, which essentially means building your self-awareness and learning how to consciously recognize behaviors that you may have. When you experience mental clarity, your capacity to have a clear understanding of your emotions, your thoughts, and the stimuli that trigger all of these experiences is increased. It becomes easier for you to understand yourself and comprehend both your instinctive responses and your rational responses because you are able to see yourself through a clearer lens.

When you experience mental clarity, you are experiencing life through mental alertness that free of stress. Because it is stress-free, you can see things as they are, rather than through your own inner perceptions that may result in you shaping the world around you in an unrealistic manner. As a result, mental clarity will also help you establish things like the ability to be unbiased or to rationally respond to situations without being hijacked by your emotions.

You develop mental clarity through a series of mental and physical practices that can help you overcome the typical triggers that lead to a lack of mental clarity in the first place. This includes mentally learning how to overcome emotions and stressors that may prevent mental clarity and physically creating a space around you that does not stimulate additional stress and mental clutter.

To begin mastering your mindset to reduce mental clutter, you need to start learning how to manage and overcome stress. The three ways that psychologists most recommend doing this is through developing a routine, learning how to tap into "flow," and preventing yourself from multitasking. Routines are particularly powerful when combined with the abstinence from multitasking because they help you get into a system where you know exactly what you need to do and when. This results in you staying focused and on-task longer because you know exactly what you need to be doing and you trust that there is enough time in your day for you to achieve everything, so you stop trying to do it all at once. At first, getting into a routine will be challenging as you are likely already used to being all over the place and living in mental chaos, but as you begin to foster a daily routine that does not require you to multitask, it will get easier. In regard to getting into your "flow" state, both having a routine and staying on track with one specific task at a time will help you get into the flow and find your groove in getting things done.

To begin mastering your physical environment for the sake of developing mental clarity, the task is quite simple: declutter. You need to maintain a clean and welcoming environment that does not have too much for your eye to focus on or look at, as this helps keep your mind clear as well. By keeping your environment clean and relaxing, you can ensure that you will not be overwhelmed by environmental distractions that may prevent you from getting focused or staying focused. This includes keeping your home clean and comforting while also favoring other environments that are more comfortable and relaxing as well, including when you go out for entertainment. Of course, enjoying upbeat and busy environments from time to time can be a great way to build excitement; spending too much time in these environments can further increase stress and decrease your mental clarity. Seek to spend more of your downtime in environments such as relaxing cafes, calm restaurants, quiet parks, and other comforting places. You should spend time in these places with friends when hanging out, but also on your own so that you can break away from the hustle and bustle of your daily life to get some calm and peace away from your normal routines. This really helps to detach your mind from everyday stress and keep you more in tune and in sync with your body and mind.

Learning to Remain Unbiased

Being biased means that you are approaching life with a very specific set of opinions and perceptions on the world around you and that you are attempting to fit everything in your life into these perceptions. Anytime something happens in your world, you will be quick to judge it and attempt to formulate an opinion on it, which can quickly result in you generating unnecessary suffering. Think about it: how often has something happened around you that should have been irrelevant to you but generated a significant amount of stress in your life for no apparent reason? Maybe your friend did something when you were nowhere near them, and it had no impact on you whatsoever, but you were upset with them because of the very fact that they would do such a thing. Or, maybe a coworker didn't get something done the day before, so you had to do it and you were angry about it because, even though it didn't change the fact that you still had to be at your job for 8 hours, now you had one more thing to do. Perhaps your judgment and anger get even more trivial sometimes, like when you are driving and you see one person cut another person off, and you become angry because of an ignorant driver on the road. Even though they had absolutely no impact on you, your judgment on their behavior resulted in you growing angry with them and produced unnecessary suffering on your behalf.

In our society, we are not taught about how we can detach from our opinions and perceptions and see the world through unbiased eyes which often results in us developing feelings of anger, jealousy, and resentment towards other people. The problem is, these feelings are completely unnecessary because, in many cases, the experiences that lead to these emotions do not even concern us, and if they do, the impact they have on us is minuscule.

Two things work against us that impact our tendency to be biased towards negativity in our lives: negativity bias and a society of individuals who are not consciously aware of their own negativity bias.

Negativity bias is a survival mechanism that allows us to recall negative experiences that we have had so that we can avoid having them again. From a survival standpoint, negativity bias makes a lot of sense and can be highly useful in helping us avoid, say, getting eaten by a cougar in the middle of the forest. Unfortunately, it doesn't do us much good living in a society where we are mostly safe from the world around us. Instead, it often leads to us feeling intensely negative about things that do not really matter, and it can grow into full-blown pessimism if we are not taught to manage our negativity bias.

What happens when you have an entire community of people not managing their negativity bias is a community of people who are negative and pessimistic. This negativity spreads like wildfire and can cause several people to feel far more intense feelings of negativity and anger within just a few minutes. You have probably experienced it yourself: when you walk into your office and your boss is in a bad mood, and then suddenly the entire office building seems to be in a bad mood as well, including yourself. Negativity bias can produce serious negative consequences when people are not consciously aware of what it is and how it is negatively impacting their lives.

The best way to remain unbiased is to become self-aware and start paying attention to how your own negativity works and how you may be contributing to your own negative feelings. By recognizing your behaviors and the way that you contribute to negativity in your own life, you can start understanding how it impacts you and how your own perceptions are impacting your mood. As a result, you can start opening your mind to seeing your daily experiences from all angles and recognizing that nothing is ever as it seems, even if you have plenty to convince you otherwise. Try and see things from everyone's perspective and, as you do, detach from your own perspective enough to be unbiased from your experiences and perception.

As you do, suddenly that person that cut you off becomes a human in your mind, and you realize that they may just be someone who is rushing to the hospital to have their baby or home to see their family that they miss so dearly. Your boss who was previously arrogant and selfish may just be someone who came from a tough youth and had to fight their way to the top and has never let go of their fighting spirit.

Your friend who made a poor decision when they were out on the weekend is just a human who decided for themselves, and one that had absolutely no impact on you whatsoever. And you, you become a human who cares deeply about everyone else, to the point that you have let their actions impact your own emotions. Everyone becomes a lot more *human* when you choose to release your bias and see people, and situations, for what they truly are.

Rationally Responding to Passionate Emotions

Emotions can be *intense,* and in a person who lacks mental toughness, they can be crippling. In the psychological field, when intense emotions overcome someone and cloud their rational judgment, it is known as "emotional hijacking." Emotional hijacking is most common in people who lack the ability to remain unbiased and see things rationally, so they end up experiencing intense, passionate emotions that are difficult to navigate through. This is where stoicism comes into play: it emphasizes the importance of handling these intense, passionate emotions through the power of mental resiliency and toughness.

Learning how to respond rationally to your emotional responses takes time as it requires you to learn first how to begin changing your instinctive response to emotional experiences. For example, when you experience sadness, it is likely that you have an instinctive habitual response to that sadness that begins occurring almost immediately after the sadness is triggered. Maybe you begin crying, even if it is just a small amount of sadness, or perhaps you find yourself getting angry because you were raised to believe that sadness was something to be ashamed about. This type of immediate response can trigger an even more intense emotional response, all of which launches as a habit of the initial emotion being triggered. For that reason, the first step in developing freedom from your intense and passionate emotional responses is to start by understanding what triggers are causing them. When you can begin to identify your emotional triggers, you can start to pinpoint the exact moment that your habitual emotional responses are preparing to launch and you can interrupt them with a more conscious response.

Say you are at work one day and your boss lost a piece of paperwork that you are *sure* you gave them, but they insist that it is your fault that the piece is missing. Perhaps this is a very important piece that places a lot of pressure on both you and your boss, and the fact that it is missing and you cannot prove that it was not you who lost it means that your job could be on the line. A stressful experience like this could easily trigger you to become angry and, if you were acting passionately, it could result in a massively angry outburst. This outburst would add to the stress of the situation and may result in you losing your job because of how unprofessionally you handled yourself during a challenging experience. As a result, you would experience even greater discomfort and anger, as well as a significantly higher amount of suffering due to your own emotional response.

If, however, you were to recognize that intense anger is starting to boil up and you were to choose to respond differently, you may start regaining rational control over yourself before your emotions boiled over. You might then find yourself being able to level out your emotions and support your boss in finding or replacing the important paperwork so that you could both calm down from the stress of the experience and move on. It may seem unreasonable for you to have to correct your bosses mistake. However, if you weigh the pros and cons of both sides of the situation, you may realize that this is a significantly smaller amount of suffering than if you were to react emotionally.

Building Mental Resiliency

Part of mental toughness is being able to bounce back from challenging situations time and again. Lindsay Teague Moreno, a self-made millionaire, claims that her mental resiliency is exactly what got her to her entrepreneurial success. In her words, she claimed that she could be at work all day and get knocked down over and over all day long and still show up the next day and walk in the door ready to work. Individuals who have experienced any capacity of personal or professional success in their lives will always tell you that their ability to get back up and try again was the exact reason for their success. Our society even has a series of quotes around this very topic that are intended to help people recognize the value of mental resiliency. Quotes like "get back on the horse," "fall seven times, get up eight," "no hoof, no horse," or "it's just a bad day, not a bad life" are all meant to remind us about the power of our mental resiliency. Still, not everyone is fully aware of how to tap into this resiliency and actually use it to change their lives.

In stoicism, building mental resiliency means that you can allow yourself to bounce back from intense emotions quicker, allowing you to regain ration in even the most challenging of situations. As you begin to develop your mental resiliency, you will find that enduring emotionally trying situations becomes easier because you are capable of bouncing back emotionally. In many experiences we have in life, a lack of mental resiliency can lead to an increase in emotions because, not only do you find yourself facing emotional struggles, but you also find yourself ill-equipped to overcome them. As a result, you may fear the feeling of being trapped in your emotions or unable to overcome them. This fear or uncertainty does not rise because you truly cannot overcome your emotions, but because you are not yet equipped with what you need to do so, which leaves you feeling fearful. Rationally, you cannot think of how you can reasonably get through your emotional struggles, so as your emotions grow, your irrational mind kicks in and leaves you feeling as though these emotions may never change. For this reason, mental resiliency will help you not only overcome life challenges but also emotional challenges and develop your stoicism more strongly.

Building the type of mental resiliency that is going to allow you to bounce back from challenging times takes patience and practice, but if you keep at it, you will discover that it's actually not as hard as it may seem. In fact, in most circumstances, it is simply about shifting your perspective and realizing that not everything is as challenging as it may seem. When you can begin considering your life through a particular perspective that actually serves your growth, rather than one that keeps you trapped in the belief that you can't make it happen, mental resiliency becomes easier. This is because you begin looking at things with the desire to grow through them and succeed, rather than feeling trapped in fear of the challenges that you face.

Creating this perspective takes practice as you begin conditioning yourself to look for ways forward, rather than admitting defeat and choosing to stay where you are at. This may sound simple enough, but for many people, the practice of changing their habitual thought patterns is particularly challenging, especially if you have never consciously taken control over your thoughts before. The best way to do this is to begin by having a mantra that you can carry with you to support you in staying clear on your goals so that you can regain mental control over your experience. Your mantra can be anything from "I choose not to react until I decide how to respond" to "I can overcome this." Once you choose a mantra, repeat it to yourself every time you face challenges in your life, particularly those around your emotions. This way, you can start conditioning yourself to endure trying times so that you no longer find yourself trapped in the false beliefs of being incapable of overcoming challenges.

After repeating your mantra to yourself, you need to begin consciously changing the way that you are viewing the situation so that you can take yourself out of victim mentality and start putting yourself into a victor mentality. A common tool for reframing challenging experiences is swapping out "Why is this happening to me?" to "How is this happening for me?" or "What can I learn from this?" When you begin to look at situations with the desire to either develop a greater understanding around them or to develop a solution, it becomes easier for you to bounce back. This is because your mind becomes focused on how you can move forward, rather than fearful and afraid of moving forward at all.

Maintaining Your Mental Toughness in Challenging Times

One place where many life changes tend to fall flat is when we are faced with particularly difficult challenges that trigger us in all of the most uncomfortable ways possible. If you have ever tried to make major changes in your life, chances are you have found yourself completely abandoning all of your adjustments as soon as things got really challenging because you were ill-equipped for what you needed to stay on track. I don't want you going through all of the efforts of building stoicism in your life only to find yourself experiencing major setbacks when you face challenges, so I have highlighted some great tools for you to stay on track even when it's a challenge.

Step 1: Slow Down

The first thing you need to do any time you face a challenge in your life that has you wanting to jump into old patterns and conditioning is to slow down. When you slow down, you give yourself the capacity to ease up on your emotional reaction and restore your ability to make a rational response to the situation at hand. Sometimes, when you are really in the heat of things, drawing back on your passion can be quite challenging, and you may find yourself struggling to stay aligned with your new stoic ways. In these situations, you may do best to completely remove yourself from the situation for a few minutes before returning with a clearer, more rational frame of mind. If you are pressed on time, a simple few minutes in the bathroom intentionally calming down and gaining some perspective over the situation can help you improve your response when you head back into the friction of a passionate situation.

If you have more time, consider slowing down your approach altogether and breaking it down into smaller steps. By paying attention to the next step, and then the next step, and then the next one, you prevent yourself from looking too far out into the future and give yourself time to make better choices *now*. You also give yourself the opportunity to see that the situation is not as large or scary as it may have seemed in the first place, which can draw back on some of the feelings of fear and frustration and allow you to address it with more rational thinking.

Step 2: Get Some Perspective

Once you have slowed the situation down, you need to get some perspective around it. Start by getting some perspective on how big the situation truly is so that you can remind yourself that virtually nothing is impossible to face, even if it seems gigantic and scary early on. Instead of allowing yourself to sit and be intimidated by the challenges that you face, sit and spend some time trying to understand them and trying to reframe them for yourself. Focus on how you can frame the challenge so that it seems manageable and achievable, rather than overwhelming and scary.

Then, go on to start searching for ways that you can overcome the challenge or even parts of the challenge as soon as possible. If you do not have all of the answers yet, start in the areas that you understand and move on from there. This way, you can at least get started and begin achieving success in overcoming your challenge. As you go along, you will likely learn everything you need to overcome your challenge even further, thus allowing you to move forward completely. Before you know it, your challenge will be a thing of the past and you will have successfully overcome it.

Step 3: Ask for Help

If you are really struggling with a challenge or if you do not have the answers you need to proceed, it is never wrong to ask for help in overcoming your challenge. Reaching out for someone who knows how to help you with your specific challenge is a great way to learn what you need to move forward successfully. Whether you need a counselor to help you manage your emotions, a coach to help you manage your time or your business strategies, or a friend to help you manage your thoughts, there is always someone out there who can help you. Simply be willing to reach out and know what it is that you need, and you can feel confident that someone will be on the other side to help you. Remember, asking for help is not a sign of weakness, but recognizing that we need help is a demonstration of strength.

Chapter 3: Discipline of Self

After you have built your foundation of mental toughness, you need to build your discipline of self. This discipline is going to help you continue building your mental toughness and conditioning yourself to use that mental toughness to develop your stoicism. As you develop your self-discipline, you will discover how you can start managing yourself through challenging emotional experiences, as well as how you can create a life that avoids unnecessary suffering. This is going to enable you to have the resiliency and knowledge to help you choose to respond to situations, rather than to react to challenging situations as they arise. Through this, you will be more stoic in your responses, which will lead to less suffering and greater growth in your life both personally and professionally.

In this chapter, we are going to focus on areas of self-discipline that are going to directly support you in managing your emotions better, as well as reducing the amount of unnecessary suffering you may face directly through your actions. This way, you can start living a life that does not produce unnecessary challenges and a life that has a greater self-discipline in facing the challenges that arise.

Accepting Yourself

Self-acceptance is one of the most powerful forms of self-discipline that you can embrace because it allows you to accept yourself as you are and stop putting pressure on yourself to be someone that you are not. Self-acceptance does not mean that you are not willing to look for opportunities to grow, but instead, that you are willing to accept when you are not embodying the growth that you wish to represent in each moment. When you accept yourself, forgiving yourself for mistakes and accepting that you are human and experience human experiences, including emotions, become significantly easier because you stop resenting yourself for your human nature. This means that any time you make a mistake, fail to move forward due to a lack of understanding, or experience an unwanted emotional outburst or setback, you accept yourself in spite of what happened. With true self-disciplined self-acceptance, you accept yourself even in the times when you feel that you have acted unacceptably because you accept yourself for exactly who you are in every single moment.

Being able to accept yourself this deeply can be challenging, especially in a society where we are often taught that we are only able to be accepted when we act or behave in a certain way. However, it is imperative as it allows you to accept yourself and love yourself even when you act 'wrongly,' which prevents the unnecessary pain and suffering associated with *not* accepting yourself. It also ensures that you are willing to move on quicker because you do not hold yourself back through your own contempt and hatred towards your unacceptable actions and behaviors. So, not only does it allow you to prevent the unnecessary suffering of a lack of self-acceptance, but it also allows you to prevent the unnecessary suffering of everything that follows that lack of self-acceptance.

Accepting yourself deeply and unconditionally takes time and practice, but it is essential if you want to experience true growth in your life. For that reason, you need to devote time every day to intentionally affirming your self-acceptance to yourself and your willingness to stay in acceptance with yourself even during challenging times. Of course, this is not always easy to achieve, so you are going to need to practice this every single day, even when it feels challenging or you feel as though you truly do not accept yourself at that moment. Realize that the thing you are not accepting of when you make a mistake in your life is not *you* personally, but your behavior and the consequences of that behavior. When you realize that you yourself are not the unacceptable one but your behavior was, it becomes easier to realize that you are still worthy of acceptance, even if your behavior was out of alignment.

Another great way to start building self-acceptance is to start journaling every time you feel that you are struggling to accept yourself. Writing down the reasons why you feel like you do not accept yourself and spending some time understanding your own true feelings and experiences can help you move beyond your unwillingness to accept yourself. This is because often when you see what you are thinking on paper, you realize how unkind or unrealistic it is, and it becomes easier for you to disown that way of thinking. You grow to realize how it is not serving you or how it is actually harming you, and you discover that there may be a better way: such as choosing self-acceptance.

Accepting Things Beyond Yourself

Acceptance with self-discipline needs to go beyond self-acceptance and into the acceptance of everything and experiences that you have in your life, too. When you live a life where you frequently do not accept what is happening around you or the people who you are surrounded by, it can present many unnecessary experiences of suffering. This suffering can arise because you feel intense emotions to everything around you on a consistent basis, for a myriad of different reasons. For example, perhaps, because you are unable to accept your family as they are, you find yourself angry and annoyed every time you are in their presence. As a result, you are unable to enjoy the presence of your family even if you genuinely feel as though you love them, which can lead to suffering. You may feel as though you are obligated to see them due to your love for them and your familial connection, or because you will experience alternative forms of suffering if you do not. So, whether you choose to see your family and suffer in their presence or avoid your family and suffer in their absence, you will still experience suffering because of your own inability to accept your family.

The same can be said for your job, your financial well-being, your home, your community, and anything else that exists beyond yourself. When you cannot accept the things around you, your surroundings become a constant source of discomfort and pain which can lead to you having constant feelings of depression, disappointment, frustration, and anguish. Learn to accept situations and people as they enable you to bypass unnecessary suffering and begin cultivating a deeper sense of appreciation for the life that you have. As a result, you cannot only avoid suffering but also cultivate contentment through the very act of acceptance.

Learning how to accept the things beyond you starts with you discovering how you can tolerate the presence of various things, experiences, or people without taking everything so personally. When you realize that other people's actions or behaviors are not an attack on you personally, as well as with your circumstances and things in your environment, acceptance becomes easier. This is because you can realize that the world around you is not victimizing you, but instead, you are simply experiencing it. It is within your mind that the victimizing begins when you genuinely believe that every person, thing, and experience is intended to be a personal attack on you.

You can also develop a greater sense of acceptance by recognizing that, in many cases, your perception of other people has something to teach you about yourself. By seeking out what that lesson may be, you offer yourself the capacity to understand why you are so bothered by others and how you can stop choosing to not accept others based on who they are, or circumstances based on what they are. See why you are so deeply bothered and why it feels as though you cannot overlook these things, and choose to find ways to overlook them and move on anyway. You always have a choice in your life, and you can choose to either let go of great friendships over small things or to accept things as they are and find a way to tolerate the fact that you cannot control others around you.

Maintaining Virtue and Kindness

Stoicism is not just about tolerating those around you and ignoring your own emotions, but rather, it is about learning how to manage those emotions and find more kind-hearted ways through them. For example, if you experience anger towards a certain situation, choosing to express that anger through words and finding a resolution calmly would become your goal. This way, you can experience your anger, discover a solution, and move forward from your anger without engaging in behaviors that can cause major consequences for both yourself and those around you. In stoicism, this is the ultimate goal because, through proper and intentional management of your emotions, you can avoid engaging in major blowouts that can lead to further emotional struggles such as guilt and shame.

In life, your virtue refers to your behaviors and how they reflect your moral standards in life. If you are someone with great virtue, then you are someone who has high morals and who lives up to those morals through your behaviors and your actions. Historically, virtue also reflected ones' purity physically and mentally, so it often involved maintaining your virginity until marriage so that you would be completely pure. In modern days, a virtue often coincides with kindness because people who possess high morals believe that those around them deserve to be treated with kindness and respect, so being kind to others is a symbol of virtue in a person.

Maintaining your own virtue and kindness truly is self-discipline because we are often compelled to behave in ways that abandon virtue and kindness based on the experience of our emotions. When you experience frustration, for example, you may become snappy and harsh in your tone, making everyone around you feel as though you are not respecting them and their feelings. Chances are, this reaction is not intentional or even conscious; it is a habitual emotional response to having your feelings triggered in a particular way. Likely, it stems from not having a strong education around how to handle your emotions properly.

When you want to develop and maintain your virtue, your goal is to begin identifying what morals you desire to live by and seeking the opportunity to live by those morals in your life every single day. Common morals include or relate to humility, kindness, abstinence, chastity, patience, liberality, and diligence, which are the opposites of the seven deadly sins that are commonly taught in many religions. These virtues ultimately seek to shape people into being individuals who are willing to show up and serve not only themselves but their communities by supporting everyone around them in living in a positive life. When you consider these virtues, consider what they mean to you and how they impact your life, and then declare that you are prepared to begin living by these virtues every single day. Then, every single day, do what you can to live in alignment with these virtues and be willing to accept yourself when you do not. As you continue practicing and reminding yourself of these virtues, you will find that it becomes much easier for you to grow as a person and to maintain your virtue and kindness along the way.

Making Peace with Your Past

Many people abandon self-discipline due to guilt, shame, and residual fear that they hold onto from their past experiences. It is not uncommon to live a life where you are shaped by your past, particularly as humans who have the capacity to remember it and to remember the emotions that coincided with these memories. One of the vices of evolution is that, in being able to remember our past so that we can improve our chances of survival, we can also remember our past to the point that it retriggers trauma within us on an ongoing basis. Making peace with your past by healing unresolved traumas and challenges and accepting what you cannot change is a powerful way to release yourself from the grips of your own history and permit yourself to move forward

When you choose to move forward without letting your past hold you back, it becomes easier for you to accept yourself more wholly and completely, including who you were in the past and who you desire to be in the future. You stop denying yourself the right to a joyful and evolutionary future because you no longer punish yourself for your experiences in the past. So, it becomes easier for you to possess even greater levels of virtue, kindness, acceptance, and mental toughness. Thus, making peace with your past directly supports your ability to develop your stoicism and become a more ethical person as a whole.

Making peace with your past takes a significant amount of emotional healing, and may not always be ideal to do on your own. Healing from your past is going to require you to personally go within and discover what needs to be healed and do some of the work yourself, while also reaching out for help whenever help is needed. By reaching out for help, you ensure that you have the support and acceptance needed to help you overcome challenging experiences in your life and grow as a person. However, the reality of inner healing is that no one else can do it for you, so you are going to need to be willing to endure the emotional aspects of healing on your own. As you do, you will find that accepting your past becomes easier because you come to peace with everything that has happened to you and how you have been impacted by various people and experiences in your life. This type of healing brings closure to painful experiences, which is often all that is needed for us to make peace with our pasts.

Overcoming Procrastination and Distractions

One of the biggest ways that people generate pain in their own lives, aside from being unwilling to accept the things beyond their control, is procrastination. Procrastination can be caused by many things, and no matter what the root cause is, it virtually always causes severe setbacks and troubles for the people who do not teach themselves to overcome this unhelpful behavior. From causing a significant amount of unnecessary stress for having to catch up last minute to causing guilt and shame for things not being completed on time, many negative setbacks can be derived from procrastination.

Overcoming procrastination in your own life requires you to start by getting to the root cause of your procrastination and finding ways to bypass that root cause so that you can get past it. In many cases, the root cause is emotional. With procrastination, you may be procrastinating something because it brings you pain, or because the alternative brings you joy. For example, you may procrastinate healing from your past because revisiting parts of your past is a painful experience for you, so you are afraid to get into it. Alternatively, you may procrastinate getting a task done for work because watching TV brings greater joy than crunching numbers or putting together presentations.

By discovering what it is that you are being motivated by more (the avoidance of pain or the desire for comfort), you can begin finding ways to work through the work that needs to be done. Some ideas include going through the process slowly so that it is not too overwhelming, breaking it down into manageable steps, or rewarding yourself for achieving success along the way. These types of small adjustments to your approach can make it easier for you to stop avoiding the process so that you can get it done and get on with your life. Once you have determined what adjustments you want to make, the last thing you have to do is get up and actually get started. For some people, this will be plenty to help them get up and get past their behavior of procrastination.

For others, these may not be enough to keep them on track, and they may find themselves backsliding into procrastination rather quickly. If you are this type of person, you need to find a way to implement some strategies to help you avoid procrastination even after you have already started. One great strategy is to find out what is distracting you or tempting you to procrastinate and avoiding that distraction as much as you possibly can. Another way is to implement a distraction time limit for yourself, as this may be more affected for people who truly cannot overcome distractions in their lives. If you are someone who gets distracted and genuinely struggle to get focused again after even a minor distraction, first off, realize that you are actually extremely normal. Recent studies have suggested that the average attention span of a human is 2.5 seconds before they become distracted once again and need to regain focus. By the way, that means that our attention span is now shorter than that of a goldfish if you were wondering!

By giving yourself a distraction break every now and again, which is simply one to three minutes to engage in a distraction and get it out of your system, you relieve your mind off the urge to get distracted and help yourself regain focus. If you find that you are getting distracted *a lot*, consider starting with frequent one-minute distraction breaks and then spacing them out further and further so that you can train yourself to increase your attention span. This way, you can condition yourself to avoid distractions without expecting yourself to be able to change your behaviors overnight completely.

Moving in Alignment with Your Goals

Another method of self-discipline that is seldom taught, but highly necessary in reducing the amount of suffering that you experience in your life, is learning how to move in alignment with your goals. Our modern society has been largely built on following a "cookie cutter" lifestyle for a long time, which means that many people are doing what they *should* be doing and are experiencing no joy or satisfaction out of it. People are pursuing jobs that they should be pursuing, getting married and having kids because they should be, engaging in hobbies because they should be, and ultimately building entire lives around the word "should." These days, there is a popular saying that goes: "Don't should all over yourself" and I think it is highly applicable here.

Doing everything in your life because you believe that is what you should be doing and because you are afraid of doing things differently only leads to you being unhappy and depressed in the long run. This is because, as humans, our emotional side needs to be nourished and taken care of and you simply cannot do that if you are constantly doing what you "should" be doing. Instead, you will find that you are building an entire life that you don't particularly care for and, because of that lack of caring, you struggle to generate motivation to actually make it happen. This all spirals into deep levels of disappointment and frustration which can ultimately lead to you living an unfulfilling life and suffering far more than you need to be.

If you want to experience true freedom and joy in your life, as well as the inner strength required to minimize your suffering, you need to start moving in alignment with your personal goals. Not only will this help you feel more fulfilled, but it will also bring a renewed sense of positivity into your life which will make acting in alignment with stoicism far easier. When you are generally a happy person, dealing with your challenging and passionate emotions becomes easier because they are not piling up and causing you to feel an intense need to release them.

You can move in alignment with your goals by determining two primary goals for yourself: who you want to be in life and what you want to have in life. By determining what these goals are, you can start setting personal rules for yourself to help you move in alignment with these goals. For example, if your goal is to be a stoic person, you will want to set rules for yourself that you will only behave in ways that cultivate your stoicism and that support you in experiencing less overall suffering in your life. If your goal is to have more money and a better house, then you would begin behaving in ways that allow you to save more money and work towards acquiring your better home.

When you set goals for yourself and you begin moving towards them, every time you see yourself making successful progress in your life, you start to feel more empowered and motivated to keep going. This can add an enriching and fulfilling feeling into your life that supports you in being happier overall. Through this, your life becomes less about suffering and more about creating one that makes you happy to wake up and enjoy your day to day experience. Many benefits can come from following personal goals, both in terms of materialistic goals and goals for yourself and your personal growth.

Chapter 4: Discipline of Action

Now that you have the inner strength and personal power required to begin moving your internal processes in alignment with stoicism, it is time for you to start bringing stoicism into your discipline of action! Your action is where you begin to allow your inner thoughts and processes develop so that you can start actually behaving stoically. This is where stoicism really comes into play because your stoic actions and behaviors will begin changing your life as you enforce them and embody them going forward. Through disciplined actions, you are going to start behaving in a way that shows emotional constraint, allowing you to use your emotions effectively, and that is ethical towards yourself and those around you.

In this chapter, we are going to discover what disciplined actions are, how they align with stoicism, and what specific actions you need to begin disciplining to embody a stoic lifestyle. Remember, stoicism heavily relies on ethical behaviors that align with virtue and morality, so your goal here is to begin acting in an ethical way that aligns with high morals. Through this behavior, you are not only going to increase your ability to embody stoicism, but you are also going to quite literally change the way that you engage with the world around you beyond your own inner thoughts and experiences.

Remember, changing behaviors like this can be quite a daunting task because you are going to be changing nearly everything about yourself likely. Since most modern humans are still highly driven by emotions, teaching yourself to become more driven by rational thought and reason without losing the value of your emotions can take time. You are truly going to be conditioning yourself into becoming a new person, which takes consistent time and practice. Furthermore, you may find that now your stoic behaviors are moving into your physical actions, the people around you start treating you differently. Those who are not benefiting from your changes may attempt to push you back into your old habits, and those who appreciate your new adjustments may start gravitating towards you in a higher degree. This means that your circle of friends and acquaintances may change as you, too, change in a rather drastic manner. That being said, deep acceptance of yourself and those around you as well as an unwillingness to revert to old behaviors will be essential in helping you completely embrace the discipline of action.

Controlling Your Emotional Passion and Expression

Where true stoicism comes into play, and not the exploitation of it that was encouraged by those who profited off of emotional repression, is when you learn how to actually control your emotional passion and expression. Through controlling your emotional passion and expression, you teach yourself to harness your emotional power and turn it into a productive tool to help you advance further in your life. For example, anger around activism that is not turned into blind rage can instead be used to passionately change people's opinions and support the true cause of the activist. Passion about the need for more love in your relationship can be harnessed to produce changes in your relationship, rather than to produce jealousy and anger around the fact that changes are not being made. When you learn how to control your emotional passion and expression, you allow yourself to use that passion alongside rational thinking to fuel the actions required to make changes in your life or the lives of those around you.

Learning how to control your emotional passion is not only a form of emotional intelligence, but it is also a form of ethical behavior. By that I mean, stoicism believes that we should always act ethically no matter what we are doing, whether it is professional or personal. How you treat people, for example, should be ethical or of high moral standards so that you always treat people with the utmost respect and kindness in all circumstances. Behaving in this way ensures that you are always doing right by yourself and by those around you, which in turn earns you greater respect and appreciation from others.

If controlling your emotions and harnessing their power to stimulate change were easy, we would all be doing it. So it goes without saying that the balancing act of being able to experience emotional passion without expressing it intensely is challenging. Learning how to regain control over yourself amidst intense emotions requires you to slow down the experience and intentionally work with your emotions in a controlled manner. You can do this by noticing the moment an emotion begins to grow in intensity and review what the goal of that particular emotion is. For example: if you are jealous in your relationship, your goal is to develop security; if you are angry with how someone is treating you, your goal is to be treated better; and if you are grieving about a loss that you have endured, then your goal is to heal the pain.

Recognizing what your goal is with any particular emotion allows you to avoid becoming the victim of that emotion, and instead, become a person who can reasonably work his/her way through the emotion. It also prevents you from turning that emotion into a larger point of trauma or emotional suffering and enables you instead to use it to reduce your suffering overall. The next step is to begin acting in a way that works in alignment with your emotion's goal rather than your emotion itself. This is where the intense act of self-discipline comes into play: in holding yourself back from emotionally reacting and following through with your goal-based actions instead. In this situation, slowing down your approach to your resolution as much as possible will allow you to regularly check in with your goal and ensure that you are acting in alignment with it. If at any time you move out of alignment with your goal, then you will be checking in often enough to regain control over your emotions and adjust your approach.

Practicing emotional control and expression frequently enough will really be the key to developing deep control over your emotional expression. They say that you need to practice something at least 1,000 times before you completely master it, so trust that every time you have the opportunity to practice the emotional control you are working towards greater success. The more intentional you become and the more serious effort you put into regaining control over your emotions, the greater control you will have in the long run.

Acting in an Ethical Manner

In the early days of stoicism, a series of ethical actions were outlined that were intended to give stoics a set of rules to live by, so to speak. These rules were fairly simple and were intended to guide people through the proper resolutions of challenging experiences that they would face throughout their lives. The Stoics called these rules "appropriate acts" or "proper functions" and they were defined by behaving in a way that adhered to what reason persuaded them to do. So, rather than being persuaded by their emotions, the Stoics aimed to be persuaded by their rational thinking mind, or reason. Stoicism aims to achieve the process of justified, rational thinking so that every action is enacted in a way that honors both parties involved and works towards achieving a higher goal, rather than an immediate emotional goal.

For things that were not inherently good *or* bad, such as health, stoics aimed to maintain their health positively which allowed them to turn the act of maintaining good health into an ethical act. This way, they could walk in one with their human nature and harmonize their lifestyles through the act of maintaining good health. Another example was through the act of sacrificing ones' property, which could either be good or bad, depending on the circumstances at hand. If the act was done because it made a good, reasonable sense to do so, then it likely aligned with stoic's virtues and morals for ethical living. If it didn't adhere to reasonable persuasion, however, then sacrificing one's property was not an act of ethical morals and therefore was considered to be "bad". For example, someone was threatening the livelihood of your family if you did not sacrifice your property. In this case, it would make rational sense to sacrifice your property to protect the lives of your family, so sacrificing your property would be virtuous and ethical. If, however, the sacrifice was being made for personal fortune and well-being but would cost your family in some large way, then sacrificing your property would not be ethical and would be out of alignment with the stoic way of living.

If you want to act in an ethical manner true to stoic nature, you need to learn how to justify things based on rational and reasonable thinking and then act accordingly. In doing so, you bring your decision-making process into the heart of reason and out of the grips of emotions which can often lead to us doing things that are completely out of alignment with the greater good. If you want to act in true stoic nature, simply ask yourself: "Is this a reasonable decision to make? Can I reasonably justify this? Will it lead me towards my true goal, or away from it?" If the answers to these questions support your decision, chances are it is a true, ethical decision that is going to support your success. If the answer is no, then chances are you are acting out of alignment with ethics, and you need to reassess your proceedings to ensure that you are acting ethically towards yourself and everyone else involved in the situation with you.

Solving Your Problems Effectively

Learning how to act ethically and with control over your emotional passion and expression will not only help you refrain from producing unwanted consequences through your actions, but it will also help you when it comes to problem-solving. People who can bypass emotional intensity and tune into their rational thinking mind are often able to get a clearer understanding of their problems and choosing actions that will support them in discovering a genuine resolve. As you continue learning how to gain more control over your emotions and how you act on them, you should also begin diving into this major benefit of being able to tune into your rational thinking mind with greater clarity and intention.

Exercising your mind for problem-solving abilities is much easier once you have gained control over your emotions and have started tapping into your reasonable thinking mind. From there, all you need to do is begin developing the habit of looking at a problem from a bird's-eye view so that you can clearly see the entirety of the problem itself. If you are experiencing a problem that involves other people, seek to understand the problem from everyone's angle and get a clear understanding of what all your goals are so that you can work towards finding a solution that serves each of your goals. If you are experiencing a problem on your own, seek to understand the obstacles that are standing in your way and put them into perspective. See them for what they truly are, avoid making them appear larger to yourself, and get clear on what it will actually take for you to reasonably overcome these obstacles in an ethical way. That way, you can start producing action steps for you to take that will help you move towards your goal without compromising your moral standards.

After you have mentally produced a solution to overcoming your goals, the next step is to actually act that solution out. Again, you are going to need to put in a lot of work towards overcoming your personal challenges such as your emotional habits that are going to encourage you to behave in the way that you have always behaved. You will need to consistently practice and remain intentional towards changing your behavior so that, over time, it grows easier for you to behave in a more constrained and intentional manner.

Once you are able to combine your reasonable thinking and controlled emotional expression into your problem-solving abilities, you will have an incredibly powerful tool in your hands. This tends to be the most challenging time to combine emotional restraint with reasonable actions as problems can bring with them feelings of fear and desperation, in addition to the other emotions that arise. Learning how to navigate through these challenging times will put your stoicism to the ultimate test, and when you navigate these effectively, you can feel confident that your stoic development is working.

Acting with Discipline in Relationships

In relationships, it can be particularly challenging to act stoically because your emotions can be so much more intense. Love is an emotion that we all crave and need, and that can bring us great suffering and pain if we do not learn how to navigate alongside the emotion of love effectively. For many, love can be one of the most overwhelming emotions to experience because it tends to sweep through your entire body and hijack your mind with no warning signs. Then, from that state of emotional hijacking, other emotions have the capacity to squeeze into your emotional hijacking and take over how you express yourself. As a result, you can find yourself being completely backward in acting stoic in relationships, even if you are managing your stoicism well in other areas of your life.

These feelings are not exclusive to your romantic relationships, either, but instead in any relationship where love or deep admiration towards another human is present. When you experience love in your life, you need to be extra cautious and considerate towards your emotions and how you may be expressing your emotions in relation to love. For example, if you are continuing a relationship because you love the other person, but it brings you both tremendous suffering, then continuing the relationship or at least continuing it in a current way may not be ideal. You may need to adjust how you are approaching the relationship or consider terminating it altogether to eliminate the unnecessary suffering of both yourself and the other person.

Acting ethically in relationships truly requires you to deeply consider how both you and the other person are being impacted and whether or not the relationship makes reasonable sense as it is. If your relationship makes sense but the actions taking place within the relationship do not, then it may be time to reconsider how you treat each other and the respect that you have for each other. If your relationship no longer makes sense, or there is no way to restore it to a state where it can stop causing hurt, then it may be time to take a break from it or terminate the relationship altogether.

Always make sure that the way you treat your loved ones is respectful of both yourself and them, and that you never allow your emotions to persuade you to behave unreasonably. Be cautious to never let love get in the way of reason by frequently checking in with your behaviors and making sure that it makes reasonable sense to move forward in the way that you are. This way, you can always treat your loved ones, including yourself, with the respect and compassion that they deserve, whether that is experienced up close or from afar.

Moving Towards Professional Goals Ethically

Another area of your life where you need to begin developing self-discipline is in your professional life. Emotions tend to hold people back when they start behaving in an emotionally-driven manner at work, whether that is conscious or unconsciously driven. For example, being upset with your boss is one thing, but taking it out on your boss through a passionate expression of emotion can result in you being seen as unprofessional and unstable. It may even result in you losing your job due to an inability to function professionally while in the workplace. It is imperative that you learn how to manage your emotions properly so that you can behave in a controlled manner during professional experiences, ensuring to yourself and everyone around you that you are stable enough to handle professional duties.

Stoicism also needs to be reflected in your relationships with people in your professional life, no matter who they may be or what role they may play in your profession. From your boss to your coworkers or even your customers, you should always be handling yourself in a professional manner that honors your high ethics and moral standards. It may seem fun and harmless to engage in inappropriate relationships, behaviors or conversations with people relating to your career, but in the long run, it may not be the best idea. You never know how these types of seemingly harmless interactions could later impact the well-being of your career and lead to you experiencing troubles in moving forward. For example, your chummy relationship with your boss may make your present work life more enjoyable, but if it is not controlled through rational thinking, it may lead to them liking you but seeing someone else as a better fit for promotion. In this case, your overly friendly relationship may not be bad enough to get you fired, but it may cost you the professional respect and consideration of your boss.

You should always consider the reasonable reality of your professional career and how your behaviors and actions are moving you towards success. If it does not make reasonable sense to behave in the way that you are behaving, even if it seems harmless on the surface, you need to begin adjusting your behaviors. This way, you are seen as professional and competent, and it is *you* who will excel faster than anyone else due to your reasonable behaviors.

Chapter 5: Achieving the Goal of Stoicism

You are officially equipped with all of the basic understanding that you need to embody to begin achieving the goal of stoicism. Hopefully, you have already begun practicing and embodying some of the teachings from earlier in this book, but if you haven't yet, do not worry: we are going to begin applying these practices right now. In this chapter, you are going to learn about what it takes for you to actually achieve the goal of stoicism and practices you can start using right away. These tools are all powerful in incorporating into your lifestyle to help you achieve the goal of stoicism one step at a time.

Making total life changes can be trying and it takes a particular degree of devotion to officially embody the goals of total lifestyle changes, including the goal of stoicism. Be sure to proceed through this chapter while applying each step at your own pace and searching for ways to incorporate it into your personal way of living. Everyone will have a slightly different take on how they personally can develop and embody lifestyle changes, so do not be afraid to make your own personalizations to these tools. As long as the heart of the tools remains the same, your application can be done in any way needed to achieve *your* goal of stoicism.

Understanding the Goal of Modern Stoicism

Let's begin by refreshing your mind on what the goal of modern stoicism truly is. You already know that the goal of stoicism, in general, is to reduce suffering by embodying an ethical way of living, but you may wonder exactly what that means or what that looks like in a modern world. After all, the world we are living in today is significantly different from the world that existed in ancient Greek and Roman times. So, let's take a deep look into what modern stoicism looks like and the goals that it aspires to accomplish.

Despite advancing a great deal in society, many humans continue to live lives that are highly steeped in stress and suffering. It has almost become a part of the societal norm to make a joke out of living the "typical modern lifestyle", which regularly involves working at a job you dislike with a boss you don't respect and doing things out of obligation instead of personal desire. Unfortunately, just because you can make light of your suffering does not mean it does not exist any longer. If you truly want to live the stoic way, you need to start taking action towards actually reducing or eliminating unnecessary suffering in your life so that you can begin living a life of greater emotional freedom.

In modern life, this looks like finding a way to accept your life as it is right now and setting goals to improve your life so that you can start experiencing greater joy and freedom. Perhaps for you, this looks like accepting your present career and the fact that you cannot get what you want from it and setting the goal to pursue a career that you are more passionate about. Or, maybe it is learning how to accept your family as they are and learning to set new boundaries so that their behaviors no longer personally affect you, allowing you to enjoy their company more without being hurt by them so much. It may even require you to terminate some friendships and relationships and begin setting higher standards on how you are willing to let others treat you and how you are going to treat others so that you can proceed with a better life overall.

Stoicism is an opportunity to stop letting emotions drive you into suffering so that you can begin moving forward rationally. Through reasonable thinking and problem-solving, you can stop letting your emotions lead you into believing that you are trapped and start letting your sense of reason remove you from the rut that you are currently stuck in. This will likely look like a total life transformation, particularly if you are presently living a life of intense suffering and struggle. Although the endurance of this transformation may be challenging, particularly as you lose those comforts and habits that have led to your suffering so far, the outcome will be more than worth it.

Advice from Stoics

These days, stoicism is broken down into two parts: modern stoicism and ancient stoicism. Modern stoicism is still highly driven by the teachings of ancient stoicism and the advice that these early philosophers shared with those who desired to embody and embrace the stoic way of living. While there is plenty of modern advice around stoicism making waves around the Internet, I want to provide you with some powerful and profound advice from ancient stoicism which is where it all began. Of course, this advice is going to be adjusted for the purposes of modern living, but I genuinely believe that connecting with the ancient roots of stoicism will help you embody it more accurately.

Below are five pieces of advice from ancient stoics that have been modernized so that you can use them in your modern life.

1. **Change Only What You Can**

Humans endure a great deal of suffering by generating a false sense of control over that which they cannot truly control. The belief that we can control other peoples' actions or decisions leads to us feeling a sense of suffering when our attempts at control betray us, and we do not actually gain the control we seek. As a result, we find ourselves struggling to accept the outcomes because we believe that there is either something fundamentally wrong with ourselves or something fundamentally wrong with those around us. The reality is that nothing is fundamentally wrong here, aside from the belief that you can in any way control anything beyond yourself.

Allow yourself to stop deluding yourself into believing that you can control anything or anyone other than yourself and start focusing on how you can control yourself. Pay attention to your personal responses and reactions to the world around you and start seeking opportunities to control those responses more effectively. The more you focus on changing yourself, including your perceptions, your thoughts, and your behaviors, the less unnecessary suffering you will experience through your own behaviors and beliefs.

2. **Start Living Today**

Procrastinating when it comes to creating a life that will be more fulfilling and enjoyable is one of the biggest acts of disservice that you could possibly do for yourself. Not only does it put off your ability to acquire what you desire, but it also results in you living in unnecessary suffering even longer as you attempt to uphold a lifestyle that does not genuinely light you up. Instead of putting it off, start focusing on living a better life today by choosing to accept yourself as you are and your past for what it is.

Look for opportunities to begin showing up passionately and ethically, find ways to build a life that is filled with meaning and purpose, and pursue your meaning and purpose rationally. Practice bringing your emotion into harmony with your reason and carrying yourself in a way that is respectful and kind to both yourself and those around you, and let yourself grow from there. Each day that you invest into living a better life, you add another day into it that you get to live free from unnecessary suffering and pain.

3. **Know That You Cannot Be Broken**

We have a tendency to place a lot of power into the hands of other people by believing that they can genuinely impact us through their actions. While the actions of others may impact our physical bodies and external circumstances, our souls can never be broken. The inner part of who you are will always remain intact and whole, and you can always choose to live in a way that honors this part of you. If you find yourself being abused or taken advantage of by others in your life, choose to remember that you cannot be broken and act as though you are whole and complete in spite of their behaviors. Not only will this minimize the pain that you endure, but it will also help you remain in control over your emotions and emotional expressions.

4. **"Don't burn the candle on both ends."**

There is an old saying that goes "Don't burn the candle on both ends" which essentially means that you should never try and endure more than you can reasonably handle. Without fully relaxing your mind and body and offering them the breaks that they need, you will be attempting to overdo it, and you will likely run yourself into a state of burnout. If you want to enjoy a happier and healthier life, you need to be able to maintain your physical and mental health and truly commit to the maintenance of it.

The emotional desire may be to do the things that make you feel comfortable, but the ethical and reasonable solution is to do the things that may not be as comforting now so that you can minimize your suffering later. By fiercely protecting your mental and physical health, you can maintain it for as long as possible.

5. **Focus Inward on Yourself**

Stoics believe that suffering comes from within, from our own perceptions and judgments of the world around us, and that this can lead to severe pain in our lives. For this reason, stoic advice is that anytime you experience the desire to judge someone else, you look within yourself to understand what that judgment means and where it is coming from.

If you are judging someone for their ill health, for example, look within and ask yourself why someone else's health would possibly impact you to the point of having your own personal suffering. Realize that you are not that intimately connected to anyone in your life, no matter how close your relationship with them may be, and that you are not required to suffer for the sake of others. Ask yourself why you are so attached to that form of suffering, and begin doing the inner healing and growth required to detach from suffering that is in no way relating to your personal experiences.

Daily Mindfulness Practices

A great way to achieve stoicism in your life is to begin practicing daily mindfulness practices. Practicing mindfulness is an excellent way to cultivate your self-awareness and to begin to recognize areas of your life where you may be increasing your level of suffering for no apparent reason. It also allows you to begin identifying where your emotions come into play and how they are impacting your daily living.

When you take the time to understand your emotions and how they are affecting you, as well as your actions and how they are affecting you, you can audit your life as a whole and seek out opportunities for growth.

In Chapter 6, we will discuss many areas where you can cultivate your daily mindfulness practice, but in essence, you are going to want to start as soon as possible by developing your self-awareness. Start asking yourself "How am I doing?" or "How am I feeling?" and begin honestly answering these questions to yourself. This way, you can easily begin to identify how you are honestly doing in life and what may be contributing to those feelings that you are having. In instances where you recognize unnecessary suffering, you can begin understanding why that suffering exists and how you are contributing to it so that you can start untangling the suffering. Then, you can begin approaching similar experiences in the future more intentionally and mindfully so as to reduce the amount of suffering you experience.

To paint a picture of mindfulness in your mind, and how this powerful tool can help you overcome suffering, let's take a look at an average daily experience that many people can probably relate to in one way or another. Imagine you were to wake up one morning and you walked into the kitchen to pour yourself a cup of coffee, only to find that there was no coffee left in the house because you forgot to purchase some when you went to the store. In this moment, you may feel a surge of frustration leap through you as you realize that your favorite morning routine has been interrupted by your own forgetfulness. When your spouse awakens and comes into the kitchen, perhaps you start taking your frustration out on him/her because you are feeling upset about the coffee situation. In this situation, you are not expressing mindfulness nor tuning into your rational thinking mind to recognize that you are simply upset that your routine has been interrupted, and not towards your spouse in any way. However, if you are not thinking mindfully and acting stoically, you might instead simply take your emotions out on your partner and increase the level of unnecessary suffering that both of you endure that morning. As you can see, bringing mindfulness into your daily practice allows you to keep everything in perspective, stay self-aware around your own experiences and emotions, and have the consciousness to choose differently. Rather than choosing to act on your emotions, you can consciously choose to act on your reason instead and be kind to your partner despite your own inner frustrations.

A Morning Meditation for Stoicism

A great way to start your day out and develop your stoicism is to begin your day with a morning meditation designed specifically to help you achieve the very goal of stoicism. Meditations are great exercises because they allow you to gain a deeper sense of emotional control over yourself, while also giving you time to visualize what you desire for yourself and making it easier for you to manifest that into your reality. For a stoic meditation, you will want to use both the releasing of unwanted emotions and the development of a vision to help you increase your stoic behaviors and cultivate a deeper sense of emotional self-control.

You can start your morning meditation by simply relaxing into a basic breathing meditation at first. To do this, relax into a comfortable seated position on the floor or on a meditation cushion and start bringing your awareness to your breath. As you become aware of your breath, start gently guiding your breath to become more rhythmic by breathing in to the count of eight and breathing out to the count of eight, too. Doing this will bring your body into a state of comfortable relaxation that will help you ease into your meditative state. When you begin to feel more relaxed, allow yourself to enjoy a few minutes of basic meditation where you can simply relax and enjoy the experience. During this first part of your meditation, you are going to develop your ability to ground your emotions and build your mindfulness, thus increasing the mental toughness that you can carry with you throughout the day. This is going to help you in tuning into your rational thinking more consistently as well, which will keep you in alignment with your goal of stoicism.

After you have spent some time relaxing in a state of meditation, you want to begin moving into the state of visualization. Here, you want to visualize what your day would look like if you were behaving stoically and how that stoicism might change the way your day would look. Envision yourself approaching your day with a greater sense of reason and ration, and with the desire to develop a stronger ability to control your emotions. Consider certain parts of your day that are typically emotionally charged and consider what they might look like if you were to take greater control over those situations in your life. When you can begin to visualize alternative habits or responses to the things that you encounter in your life, behaving in a new way becomes easier because you are essentially planning what your different responses would be. Furthermore, you envisioning yourself behaving in a completely new way actually builds your confidence in your ability to behave differently too, because you have already "seen" yourself doing it. Your ability to imagine your better responses and your better life actually creates the skills that you need to begin developing better responses and a better life.

Philosophical Diaries

Stoicism is largely based on philosophy and belief of life having a certain purpose and meaning, particularly relating to behaving in a certain way both towards yourself and towards others in your life. Stoicism itself already has a list of ethics and virtues that outlines what it is, but that does not mean that you cannot use a diary to begin developing your own belief around what stoicism is to you and what it means to you personally. When you begin to develop your own beliefs around what stoicism is and how it works, you can start really embodying and embracing this way of life in a personal manner. This allows you to make it yours and develop a personal passion, purpose, and reason for following this way of life and embodying it in your own everyday experiences.

Keeping a philosophical diary does not only support you in making stoicism more personal to yourself and your own interpretation, but it also supports you in discovering more about yourself. Through these journals, you can start digging into what life means to you, what you believe the purpose of life is, what morals and virtues you personally hold value for, and what you desire more of in life. These types of exploration topics will help you really develop an understanding around yourself and why you may behave the way you do and experience the emotions that you experience. For example, if you believe that a high moral standard is to respect your family and accept them deeply no matter who they are, then it may make sense as to why you grow so frustrated when they do something that you perceive to be unacceptable. Or, it may make sense as to why you struggle to relate with people who do not also hold their families to such great value in their own lives.

The more you understand yourself in this intimate way, the easier it is for you to develop your mindfulness even further and create reasons behind why you behave, think, and feel the way you do from experience to experience. As you explore yourself even further, identifying your own feelings and experiences from moment to moment becomes easier, and you can start carrying yourself more intentionally. Not only are you able to identify your actual habits and behaviors, but you are also able to identify how you can align them to work towards your overall goals because you now know what those goals actually are. As a result, you can experience greater growth in your life.

Studying the Art of Stoicism

When you make a total lifestyle change, such as by embodying the art of stoicism and using it in your daily life, one of the most valuable things that you can do for yourself is to continue studying that change indefinitely. For stoicism, this means that you want to continue studying the history of stoicism, what stoicism actually is, and how modern stoicism works so that you can begin applying that knowledge in your life more consistently. Ongoing education around lifestyle changes is one of the most powerful things that you can gift yourself with if you are truly serious about making permanent changes in your life.

The first reason why you want to continue educating yourself on these changes is that the more you know, the easier it is for you to actually apply the goal of stoicism into your life. As you continue to read more books, listen to podcasts, read blogs, and otherwise consume information about stoicism, you gain more insight as to how it can be applied in a variety of different experiences or situations that you may encounter in your life. As a result, you can more clearly understand how it works, what it means, and what it looks like in practical application. This means that when you encounter times that may be more trying on your emotions, you can start moving through the process of adapting to a more stoic approach easier.

Another reason why ongoing education is powerful is that it gives you a more dynamic understanding of what stoicism actually is. Every single person who has ever written on stoicism and who will ever write on it will approach the subject slightly different from everyone else who has approached the subject. This is because we all have slightly different interpretations of what stoicism is, why it is important, and how it should be applied into everyday life. As you continue educating yourself on how stoicism is being applied by other people, you can educate yourself on how you can further personalize it for your own experience as well. You may find that what has worked in the modern application of stoicism for others either fits great with you or does not resonate so much and you need to pursue a different understanding to help you achieve more.

As well, your deeper understanding of the core foundation of what stoicism is will help you begin to develop your own ideas around what it truly means and why it relates to your personal beliefs on life itself. In this way, your ongoing education around stoicism can stimulate you to begin formulating your own opinions and perspectives and even further embodying it into your own life in a way that genuinely fits you and your needs. Through this type of personalized embodiment, you grow a closer and more intimate connection to your practice which makes it easier for you to commit and devote to it in your life.

Lastly, your ongoing education around stoicism will keep it relevant to you. In a society where our average attention span is about 2.5 seconds long, it is not uncommon to read a great book, feel inspired, and then completely forget about everything you learned just a few days later. If you truly want to embody everything that stoicism has to offer, you need to be willing to stay devoted to your practice and continue keeping it at the forefront of your life. You need to put in the continued attention and effort into understanding what it is and deepening your connection with it so that you can keep growing and advancing alongside stoicism. Otherwise, there is a good chance that you will simply forget or it will become unimportant to you, and you will lack the ability to embody stoicism in your life.

Endurance Training

The last thing that you need to begin implementing into your life when it comes to achieving stoicism is developing an endurance. This endurance can be developed by regularly strengthening the foundation of your entire lifestyle change through consistent mental toughness building. The more you work towards increasing your mental strength and toughness, the stronger your foundation will be and the easier it will be for you to maintain your stoic lifestyle. If you let your mental toughness foundation break down, the rest of your practices are going to break down alongside it, and you are going to struggle to really embody stoicism in your life. That is why we started with mental toughness training and the practices that you need to begin embodying to develop the mental strength and resiliency that you need to succeed.

I suggest that you spend several minutes per day purposefully working towards building your mental toughness. You can do this by scheduling aside time for practicing the practices given to you in Chapter 2: Mental Toughness – Maintaining Your Mental Toughness in Challenging Times, as well as by practicing them spontaneously when they are particularly useful in life, such as when you are going through a hard time. Practicing mental toughness on a regular basis is going to help you stay strong enough to continue choosing your rational thinking mind over your emotional thinking mind during trying times, which will keep you in alignment with stoicism.

If you are having a particularly challenging time building your mental toughness, I suggest you slow down and stay focused on your mental endurance for a while. Do not push yourself into advancing into the stoic disciplines until you have developed a deeper sense of mental toughness. Although you will likely generate some success in these disciplines, if you lack mental toughness, you may see the back-and-forth of success-then-setbacks as too much and may find yourself feeling like you would rather give up than continue. This might completely throw your entire game off, which can destroy your success and leave you feeling defeated before you ever really got the chance to begin.

Instead, take your time and really focus on building a strong foundation of mental toughness first so that your disciplines are far easier for you to uphold. When your mental toughness is developed enough that you can see the benefits of your resiliency and personal strength, then you can begin moving on to developing your disciplines as they will be much easier to develop and maintain.

In addition to building your mental toughness through mental practices, I would also suggest that you begin building a physical endurance practice as well. Physical endurance will not only support you in maintaining your health, which is an important element of stoicism, but it will also help you build mental endurance as well. Physical endurance requires a high degree of mental commitment and devotion, which is what makes it so powerful in developing your mental endurance. Furthermore, the number of challenges that you will face physically in building your endurance will teach you about just how strong you are when it comes to emotional endurance, too.

Chapter 6: Daily Application of Stoicism

Finally, you have reached the point where you can begin applying stoicism into your everyday life! At this point, you have a strong enough understanding of stoicism and all of the tools in place for you to begin developing stoicism in your life, so you are now ready to begin developing daily practices for stoicism. This is where you really get to let your practice until now shine through as you get to put the "final touches" of your lifestyle change into place. Through these daily practices, you are going to really begin to see the fruits of your labors as these practices are small yet consistent, so they pack a big punch in making real changes in your life.

In this chapter, we are going to discuss *14 ways that you can begin applying stoicism into your daily life*. This may sound like a lot, but in reality, many of these practices are simply about mindset shifts that you can focus on creating and embodying every single day. As you do, the shifts of stoicism in your life will begin to manifest rapidly as your consistent application of stoic practices begins to snowball into your successful growth. So, if you are ready to finally apply stoicism into your everyday life, let's start!

Knowing Your True Freedom

The first way that you can begin embodying stoicism in your everyday life is by generating perspective around where your freedom lies and how your freedom can be achieved. Epictetus, a Greek stoic philosopher, once quoted that "No man is free who is not a master of himself." In other words, the only true way to gain freedom is to understand yourself and begin mastering yourself regarding your emotions, your reactions, and the way that you decide to live your life. Remember, of all the things that exist in this world, the only thing that you truly have any control over is yourself. When you learn how to control yourself, you experience true freedom because you learn how to end your suffering in any circumstance that you may face.

Whenever you are faced with trying situations in your life, recognize what your instinctive reaction is and pause for a moment to hold back from that immediate reaction. Instead, slow yourself down and take the time to gather control over yourself and your emotions before proceeding. This way, you can proceed with control over your emotional passion and expression, thus allowing you to begin making conscious choices and avoiding the suffering of emotional reactions. As you do this, you begin to develop a sense of control over the way you move, the actions you take, and the way that you express your emotional self. This type of self-control and emotional constraint becomes your biggest ally when it comes to rationally moving through your life and making choices that genuinely serve your overall well-being. Through this, your life somewhat turns into a game of chess where every move is clearly thought out and, if moved correctly, can bring you that much closer to achieving your ultimate goal.

If you want to experience a better life, you need to take responsibility for your own growth and begin developing your skills around your personal growth. The more you take responsibility, the more you put yourself back in control over your own experiences and the greater you can grow in life. This pause can mean the difference between creating a new future or recreating an (ineffective) historical past.

The Circle of Influence and the Circle of Concern

One of the most powerful instruments that exist in stoicism is the circle of influence and the circle of concern. When you begin to study these two circles, you start to realize that everything in your life falls into two categories: things that you can control (your circle of influence) and things that you cannot control (your circle of concern.) The things within your circle of control or influence are things that you can actually make effective change in through your own personal choices. The things within your circle of concern are things that you cannot directly control and that you have to either accept *or* reframe using things that are within your circle of influence.

The things that fall within your circle of influence include things like: where you work, what you buy, what you read, what skills you choose to learn, what people you meet, what friends you keep in your life, and what your attitude towards life is. These are all things that you can personally control either by adjusting your mindset around them or by choosing to engage more or less with them. For that reason, these fall into your circle of influence because you can directly influence them in your life.

The things that fall into your circle of concern include things like: the news, the economy, the political views of other people, the weather, natural disasters, wars, other people's lives, and other people's opinions. These types of things are completely beyond your control, so you will never be able to influence them or change them directly. Instead, you need to decide to either accept them as they are or adjust the way that you perceive them in your life so that you can accept them. In the end, your only real option towards ending suffering around your circle of concern is to choose to change your perception around these things.

Reframing Your Attitude on Death

According to stoicism, the sooner you define how you feel about death, the less you are going to fear death, and the sooner you will begin enabling yourself to live a better life. As Socrates stated, "To fear death, my friends, is only to think ourselves wise, without being wise: for it is to think that we know what we do not know. For anything that men can tell, death may be the greatest good that can happen to them: but they fear it as if they knew quite well that it was the greatest of evils. And what is this but that shameful ignorance of thinking that we know what we do not know?" Death itself is something that many modern people fear, but the fear itself needs to be addressed if you are ever going to overcome it so that you can allow yourself to live truly. Often, the fear of death is derived from the fear of not living a great enough life before death happens, and as a result, people begin to fear what would happen if they died. The common worry is "What if I die and I did not live my best life?" which can naturally be overcome by actually choosing to live your life. However, if you are so afraid of dying that you refuse to start living, then you will always live in this fear of not living your best life because you let that very fear hold you back.

Death itself is inevitable, no matter what way you look at it, so choosing to fear it will only hold you back further. This does not mean that you have to look forward to or even welcome death, but choosing to overcome your intense fear around it will help you begin living a better life in general as you will no longer fear what could happen if you did die. Instead, you choose to come to peace with the fact that the end is coming just like you choose to come to peace with the fact that the past has already happened. As such, you move forward with a greater emphasis on *right now*.

If the fear of death is really prominent for you, rather than trying to combat your fear of death, you may find that your ability to overcome the fear is quite challenging. In this case, rather than attempting to terminate the fear itself, you may instead choose to begin reframing that fear. For example: what are you more afraid of, death or never having lived? What are you more afraid of, dying young with a great life of exciting memories or dying old with a life of regret and missed opportunities? What are you more afraid of, going out and dying in a tragic accident or never having exposed yourself to the joys of living in the first place? Do you get where I'm going with this? If you cannot completely overcome your fear of dying, make your fear of dying smaller than your fear of missing out on living.

Growing Comfortable in Discomfort

Life is filled with challenges no matter what way you choose to live your life. If you choose to sit still in your life, you are going to face the challenges of having to fight as hard as you can to avoid change and experience the pain of not growing. If you choose to grow with your life, you are going to face the challenges of obstacles that come with growth and the growing pains that are inevitable along the way. Either way, you are going to experience some degree of suffering in your life, no matter what you do. However, if you choose to endure the growing pains as they come, you can assure that they are going to be much less painful than the lifelong pain of trying to stop things from changing.

Think of your life as an old school game of Super Mario: the screen is moving and you have to keep moving with it, or else, it moves and you get left behind eventually. In the case of Super Mario, your character would simply die, and you would start again with a new life. In the case of real life, you are simply going to experience more and more pressure coming against you which will require you to grow stronger and stronger to prevent it from actually hitting you. In most cases, you will grow exhausted at some point and weeks, months, or even years of missed growth opportunities will crash upon you all at once and demand serious change from you. In this case, the pressure of waiting plus the pressure of being hit with all of your life lessons at once will produce way more suffering than growing at a natural rate would have.

Growing comfortable with discomfort now means that you will only ever have to endure manageable amounts of discomfort in your life. As long as you continue moving forward, that pressure will not build up, and you will never experience the need to hold a mountain over your head while praying that it doesn't crush you when it all falls down at once. The suffering that you experience when you choose to grow instead of standing still is far less than if you were to never change at all.

Recreating Yourself as a Person

Until now, you have likely held fairly tightly to the identity of who you are as a person. You probably have an identity that you have clung to all of your life, or at least for most of your life, that has been shaped by significant memories and experiences that you have shared with other people. Maybe the combination of your Mother telling you that you were too sensitive and you crying after being bullied off the high school basketball team has left you believing that you are too sensitive as a person. Maybe your Dad telling you that you are special and your teachers always putting unique stickers on your work has led you to believe that you are more special than those around you. Whatever your belief about yourself may be, you can guarantee that it is not accurate as to who you truly are.

Psychology says that there are three elements to our identity: how we experience the world, our inner voice, and our persona that we share with people around us. Each of these parts of our identity is slightly different from the other two parts of our identity, thus leaving us with our true identity falling somewhere in between these three moving parts. When you realize this to be true, you realize that not only has your belief around your identity been wrong all this time but also that you can completely recreate those beliefs and your identity within yourself.

As you embody the goals of stoicism in your own life, seek to learn how you can embody it in a way that truly changes who you are. Rather than being a person who is heavily driven by emotion or who engages in irrational behavior, become a person who is driven by rational thinking. Reinvent yourself as the person who is reliable, trustworthy, and stable. Begin to develop trust in yourself and learn how to rely on yourself as being the one person that you can turn to when you are in need of genuine change in your life. Start building your relationship with yourself and everything in your life will change.

Embodying Your Own Philosophies

Remember your philosophy journal? Now is a great time to begin digging into it and embodying everything that you have been writing inside of that journal, including your own philosophies on what life is and what it means. When you begin embodying your own philosophies in life, you begin to create an intimate and personal connection with life itself. Rather than simply embracing what someone else says is true and believes is right, you can start embracing what you believe to be true and right for you.

If you believe in stoicism, chances are that your personal philosophies and beliefs somehow connect to stoicism as well. So, not only will this help you live more in alignment with your personal truth, but it will also help you embody a deeper connection to the stoic way of life and embrace it in a more personalized manner. Choose what your purpose is in life, discover your mission, and choose to live in alignment with your purpose and mission every single day. Seek the opportunity to make your own life and the lives of those around you better through your actions and infuse your everyday living with your purpose and mission.

When you embody your own philosophies, you not only start living life on your own terms, but you also start distributing your own knowledge and understanding more powerfully. What if people like

Epictetus, Zeno, and Socrates never shared their philosophies in life with those around them? Had this never happened, the Greek school of philosophy would have never been established and stoicism, amongst many other philosophies, would have never come into existence. It does not serve to keep your beliefs and philosophies to yourself when they can serve better when they are being shared with the world around you.

Always Work Towards Your Personal Mission

One of the goals of stoicism is to always be working towards achieving your personal mission in life. When you have identified what it is that you truly want to achieve with your life and what purpose you serve here on earth, choosing how to respond to challenging situations becomes a lot easier. With a clear vision, you can see what it is that you are working towards and you know exactly what you need to factor in when it comes to choosing the reasonable solution to move forward with. This makes navigating emotional challenges more manageable because you know what it is that you are working towards, so there is more at stake if you *don't* manage your emotions and respond stoically.

As you grow, your goals and dreams are going to change in your life, but your mission is always going to stay the same. Your mission is what it is that you want to achieve in your life overall, and it tends to remain consistent throughout your goals and your dreams. When you consistently work towards an overall mission in your life, it becomes easier for you to know yourself and handle yourself in virtually any situation that you face even unexpected or challenging ones. You automatically start considering your mission and that which matters most to you in the face of challenges and rationally thinking about how you can honor your mission and work in alignment with it while still proceeding. In the goal of stoicism, this prevents irrational emotional outbursts because you know what it is that you desire to achieve, so you are not caught in emotional turmoil with no clear understanding as to what is causing it or why. Instead, you can easily tell which of your primary missions or values has been compromised or is being threatened by the situation at hand, and you can rationally choose action steps that will help you proceed in alignment with your mission.

Be a Student of Life

Seneca, a Roman stoic philosopher, once said: "As long as you live, keep learning how to live." Being able to recognize that you are never going to know all that there is to know about life is imperative in allowing yourself to always remain open to all that life has to offer you. If you want to live your best life, you need to live a life with humility by realizing that you will always be learning, as long as you are alive. Every day will present you with new challenges, opportunities, changes, and lessons. As long as you are willing to, you can awaken to these lessons and embrace them and learn how to implement them so that each day is better than the last.

You may think that some days have nothing to teach you or find yourself feeling as though sometimes it isn't *you* who needs to embrace the lessons being presented. Trust that any time you attempt to push the responsibility onto someone else, you are not paying attention to life with an open enough mind because you are allowing your ego and emotions to cloud your judgment. You need to be willing to admit that the lessons being presented in life are also being presented to you.

If you find that you are genuinely going through your days with nothing to learn, your lesson may be that you need to challenge yourself more. Seek opportunities to learn and grow and put yourself in circumstances where you can start embracing greater challenges in your life. You may feel that being free of challenges is a blessing, but in reality, it is a sign that you are either ignorant towards everything around you or you are not doing enough to present yourself with growth opportunities. Use this as an opportunity to take responsibility for yourself and your personal growth and well-being and create your reality in a new and exciting way.

Create Happiness, Don't Dream of It

One of the biggest teachings in stoicism is that your goal is not to dream of having happiness, but to create it instead. Rather than placing your happiness into worldly things like materialism, place the development of your happiness into yourself. According to Epictetus, the less you need to be happy, the happier you are going to be because fewer conditions will need to be met for your happiness to be achieved. Learning how to master your mind is a profound way to begin generating your own happiness and taking responsibility for your own contentment.

Happiness in and of itself is an illusion; it is merely an emotion that we experience just like anger and jealousy. When you realize this, you realize that just like anger or jealousy, happiness can be triggered by small things as well. This reality means that it does not need to be so challenging for you to experience happiness and that there are no certain circumstances that need to be met for you to be happy. Stop telling yourself things like "I will be happy when I have more money" or "I will be happier when I live in a new house", and instead, start realizing that you can be happy *right now*.

Beyond creating your own happiness, learn how to create your own contentment. Happiness, like other emotions, will come and go, so developing an attachment to living in a state of happiness can be challenging in and of itself. It can make the pursuit of happiness so cumbersome that you find that you truly cannot experience happiness at all and so, you are endlessly chasing something that you simply cannot catch. Instead, realize that in some situations, you are not going to be happy, and being content is just as pleasant as being happy, as it means that you are at peace with all that surrounds you and all that you embody.

Learn How to Be Present

The power of presence has been talked about a lot in the self-help industry over the past few years, but the reality is that presence is not a new concept nor is it one that was modernized by recent trends. Instead, the power of presence is something that has been talked about and taught about for years, including all the way back in ancient Greek times where stoicism was originally developed. That being said, the modern trends in the self-help industry means that learning about the art of presence and how to practice being in the moment is widely taught about and easy to educate yourself on.

The ability to remain present is something that needs to be addressed differently for different people. The reality is that not everyone is going to have the same thought processes or approaches to their realities in the same way, which means that everyone is going to need to hear the information in a particular way for it to actually *click*. That being said, do not shy away from reading and consuming all of the materials that you need to consume around presence to help you learn about what it means and how to embody presence in your own life. In fact, fully immerse yourself in the practice because once you get it, everything will absolutely change.

When you live your life in the present moment, forgiving the past and seeing everything as a new experience is effortless because you are in *this* moment, not one that has already passed you by or one that has yet to arrive. This means that your emotions attached to previous memories and challenges in your life no longer drive you through current experiences, which prevents you from responding to things with an excess of emotional passion. For example, if your spouse forgets to change the toilet paper roll, you do not feel compelled to get angry at him/her for the past three years of things that he/she had done wrong in your eyes over one isolated incident. Instead, you recognize that it was one isolated incident you can treat it as such, without the intense emotional response that you may instinctively attempt to respond with if you are still living in the past.

Always Take 100% Responsibility for Yourself

Learning how to take responsibility for yourself is not only a way to eliminate your suffering but is also a way to promote your growth and success in life, too. When you take responsibility for yourself, you put the control of your life back into your own hands and give yourself the tools that you need to heal, grow, and change throughout life. It may feel difficult, but when you take responsibility for yourself, you take responsibility for your feelings and your behaviors, and you give yourself exactly all of the power you need to make changes in your life.

From a perspective of looking back on your past, taking responsibility means that you take ownership for any role that you may have played in any challenges that you may have faced and that you recognize that you could have done things differently. Then, it means accepting yourself for the choices you made and realizing that you did your best with the knowledge that you had. For the challenges you faced that you could not have changed, you take responsibility for the feelings that you continue to face and the way that this may continue challenging you now in your present life. By taking this type of fierce responsibility for yourself, you give yourself the power that you need to change your life by healing, accepting, and moving on from your past.

From a present and futuristic standpoint, taking responsibility for yourself means accepting the behaviors and actions that you are taking right now in your everyday life and how they are impacting you right now and the future version of yourself. This means taking responsibility for the fact that when you do things such as wake up late, you face the consequences of being late to your engagements. This means taking responsibility for the fact that when you do things such as consistently show up late, you set your future self-up for failure by making it nearly impossible for you to hold down a job or earn an income. When you take responsibility for yourself, it means that you are taking responsibility for every single thing that you do or do not do and how it impacts you now and the future version of yourself that is yet to come.

If you truly want to live in alignment with the goals of stoicism you need to be willing to take responsibility for your personal growth, your emotional intelligence, and your ability to develop your rational thinking. You need to be willing to identify areas in your life where you could improve, and then actually take action necessary in moving forward and improving your life. When you take responsibility for yourself and your behaviors, it is like giving yourself the keys to your brand new life, and you have the choice to either make it something truly amazing for yourself.

Grow Beyond Materialism

Mahatma Gandhi once quoted, "Increase of material comforts, it may be generally laid down, does not in any way whatsoever conduce to moral growth." Materialism is an attitude that can produce a significant amount of suffering in anyone's life. Materialism is a constant source of stress in many modern societies where the mindset of "more, more, more" is basically bred into people from the beginning and is continuously injected into people's minds. In Western society, people are taught that they need to purchase new things on a constant basis to keep up with everything else. Fashion, housewares, trendy toys or gadgets, and many other consumerism-style products are constantly being produced and marketed to people through the power of emotions. Marketers market to people knowing that they want to fit in, be cool, enhance social status, experience happiness, or experience the sentimental or nostalgic value that the object may be able to offer. Of course, true consistent emotional happiness and support does not come from materialistic items, so it leads to people constantly going through cycles of buying things for joy and then feeling empty when the novelty wears off. As they say, the best things in life are not things.

Rather than exposing yourself to this suffering and being captivated by your emotions that fear being left behind or ridiculed for not having the latest and greatest things, learn how to deny materialism in your life. Purchase only what you need and what you genuinely desire, and leave everything else behind. Base your emotions on things that you can control, such as your thoughts and behaviors, and not on things that you can acquire like toys and fashion accessories. This way, you always feel truly in control over your emotional well-being, and you do not feel as though you are constantly at the mercy of corporations that are profiting off of your emotional instabilities.

Be of Service to Others

True love is a powerful thing, and with it can come experiences such as true joy, true contentment, true fulfillment, and true excitement. When you experience true love in your life, it opens up a world of other opportunities that you can enjoy through that love directly. It does not only open it up for you, but it opens it up for those around you as well, who are being loved through your service. Through this, a significant amount of pain and suffering ends because you are opening yourself and others up to a world of love and gentleness. Studies have shown that when you express love and kindness to one person, it often creates a ripple effect as they then express it to someone else, and the act carries on over many people.

In life, one of the greatest things that we can do for ourselves and for others is to serve. If you put anyone in the position of being able to serve genuinely, they will always say that they feel infinitely happier and more abundant as a result of their service. At the end of the day, we are always trying to serve someone in addition to ourselves: our family members, our friends, our audiences, our coworkers, or our employees. Some people make it their life mission to serve as many people as possible, whereas others are perfectly content just serving a small number of people in their lives. No matter what, though, if you ask anyone about what is important to them, some form of service will virtually always come to their mind.

We feel best when we serve because the act of giving love aligns us with the act of receiving love, and that genuinely feels good. When you can rationally think about how love improves your life and the lives of those around you in this way and act in a rational way around love, your ability to serve and generate true sustainable love increases. As a result, your suffering decreases and your genuine overall happiness grows.

Embody the Lighter Side of Life

There is nothing humble about living a life that is overwhelmed with seriousness. Just because the goal of stoicism is to be rational and reasonable does not mean that you are not able to experience humor and comedy in your life. In fact, one of the best ways that you can grow mental toughness and develop your stoicism is by learning how to make light of challenging situations. Seeing the brighter side of things and allowing yourself to embody the lightness helps you overcome the suffering that is attached with being too serious all of the time.

People who are too serious take things personally, feel the weight of the world on their shoulders, and struggle to let go and experience true joy and happiness in their lives. They find themselves feeling trapped in the energy of seriousness, and it can weigh them down and leave them feeling pessimistic in the long run. Not knowing how to laugh and see and embody the lighter side of life is just as damaging on your soul as never allowing yourself to overcome the suffering that you have endured in your life until now.

Learn how to laugh at yourself when you make mistakes, and laugh at the irony of challenging situations when you cannot overcome them with ease. Learn how to see life as something that is light and joyful, and discover how you can smile at the things that are beyond your control. Give yourself the gift of being gentle in your perspective and your opinion, and avoid trying to make everything so heavy and overwhelming all of the time. In seeing the lighter side of life, you give yourself the ability to avoid getting weighed down by seriousness, and you start enjoying yourself once again. Rather than holding you back and keeping you feeling overwhelmed, your emotions instead become an ally that helps you lead a greater life when you learn how to experience the lighter side of life itself.

Conclusion

You have officially read the entirety of *Stoicism: A Practical Guide for Beginners to Practice Stoicism: Complete Guide of Self-Discipline, Mental Toughness, Productivity, and Mastering Confidence, Jealousy, and Anger Management, and Everything You Need to Know About Stoicism*! Thanks for making it through to end of this guidebook. Let's hope it was informative and able to provide you with all of the tools you need to achieve your goals whatever they may be.

By now, you should have a strong understanding of what stoicism is, where it stems from, and how it has evolved to serve the modern world. Stoicism is a powerful art that, when appropriately applied, can help you master one of the most valuable tools that evolution has granted us: your rational mind. By applying the lessons that were taught to us by ancient Greek and Roman philosophers, you can discover powerful ways to move through your challenges and experience greater success in your personal, social, and professional lives. Through the proper application of stoic ways of life, not only can you find the opportunity to experience greater success, but you can also help your own personal evolution along. The more you refine and harness the power of your rational mind, the more you work in alignment with the very nature of being a human being. As a result, you can tap into the entire power of the human mind and experience more of just about everything you desire out of life.

Stoicism is a powerful lifestyle that teaches you about the importance of reducing your own personal suffering through embodying an ethical way of living that values high moral standards. When you embody stoicism, you teach yourself how to harness the power of your emotions and use them to inspire yourself to respond to things with a more rational approach. Through this rational approach, you can work towards effectively achieving the goals that your emotions had in the first place without the unnecessary implication of further suffering.

Despite how far we have evolved, humans continue to find themselves falling into the temptation of satisfying their emotions immediately and suffering for that satisfaction in the long run rather than managing their emotions effectively and benefiting overall. Stoicism continues to support us in overcoming this need for instant gratification by encouraging us to embody the pillars of high moral standards and ethical living by favoring our reasonable mind over our emotional one. This does not mean that you should be ignoring or avoiding your emotions, but instead that you should be working in alignment with your nature and discovering how you can move forward with a whole approach.

As you move forward from this book, continue working on building your mental toughness and resiliency so that you can experience a stronger foundation to build your practice of stoicism upon. Teach yourself how to stay dedicated by staying consistent in educating yourself about stoicism and developing a personal practice that aligns with your stoic development, too. In the early stages, you may benefit from keeping this book handy so that you can refer back to <u>Chapter 6: Daily Applications of Stoicism</u> and inspire yourself to embody stoicism on a daily basis. At least, early on, this chapter will be handy in reminding you about how simply you can apply it in your everyday life. From learning to manage your anger at work more effectively so that you can continue to carry yourself in a productive way to learning how to accept your family and friends as they are and choosing to love them anyway, stoicism will help in many ways. The more you practice, the more this empowered way of living will have the capacity to change your complete life.

I encourage you as well to really take advantage of using your own philosophy diary where you, too, can begin discovering what life means to you and what you feel your purpose in life is. As you continue looking into your own inner studies, developing your personal mission, and sticking to it through your rational, decision-making becomes easier. In no time, you will discover just how easy it is to stick to the power of rational thinking when you have a genuine and powerful reason that inspires you to do so.

Lastly, if you enjoyed this book I ask that you please take the time to review it on Audible.com. Your honest feedback would be greatly appreciated.

Thank you.

www.ingramcontent.com/pod-product-compliance
Lightning Source LLC
Chambersburg PA
CBHW021131080526
44587CB00012B/1236